D0546044

COLOUR
PERCEPTION

A practical approach to colour theory

Tim Armstrong

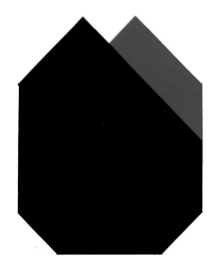

TARQUIN PUBLICATIONS

Tim Armstrong is an artist whose fascination in colour theory began in his student days when he was influenced by the paintings of George Seurat. While postgraduate at the Slade School of Art 1967–1969 he became interested in the optics of motion and colour in movement. His kinetic works were shown at the exhibition of British kinetic art "Light in Movement" at Bromsgrove, Birmingham. His prints and constructions were included in the Royal Academy Summer Exhibitions, and the Paris Salon.

From 1969–78 he lectured at Glasgow School of Art and his interest in colour developed through the medium of silkscreen printing which enabled him to employ metallic and transparent inks. Exhibitions included the Royal Scottish Academy, the Bradford Print Biennale, the American touring exhibition "Eleven British Artists", organised by the Plains Art Museum and "British Prints" at the Rourke Gallery, Minnesota. In 1977 the Scottish Arts Council commissioned him to paint two murals, each of 2000 square feet for the Gable Ends scheme in Glasgow. Since then he has worked on murals with students in Cambridge and Edinburgh, and in 1987 was commissioned to design a mural for ScotRail.

His designs are in many public and commercial collections. He now teaches in Cambridge Regional College. He continues to make and sell silkscreen prints, and has turned his interest to Oriental patterns. He is currently working on another book on visual perception.

By the same author "Make Moving Patterns", Tarquin Publications, 1982.

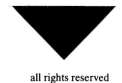

© 1991 TIM ARMSTRONG
I.S.B.N. 0 906212 74 X
DESIGN: Paul Chilvers
EDITOR: Magdalen Bear
PRINTING: STIGE, Turin, Italy

TARQUIN PUBLICATIONS
STRADBROKE
DISS
NORFOLK
IP21 5JP
ENGLAND

The Binary Window

A coloured filter absorbs some wavelengths of light and allows others to pass through. The red and cyan filters which make up the Binary Window are complementary. Those wavelengths which are transmitted by one are absorbed by the other. Folding it in half so that the filters coincide confirms this point. Almost all the light is absorbed and the window area appears dark.

This simple device provides an additional means of understanding the nature of colour and its use is suggested at several places during the course of this book.

Apart from its use in a formal, directed way, it is also valuable and interesting to play with it informally. Look through each side in turn at a wide variety of different objects and coloured pictures. By such means a greater understanding of colour and how we perceive it can be built up.

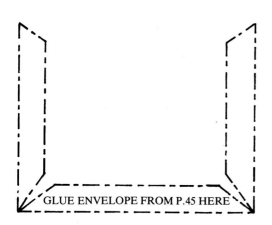

GLUE ENVELOPE FROM P.45 HERE

Contents

The Principles of Colour

Light is part of a huge range of vibration energies which is called the electromagnetic spectrum. This extends to include gamma waves and radio waves, but only a tiny section is visible to the human eye. Natural white light is a mixture of the visible wavelengths which run from about 380 nano-metres at the limits of violet to about 760 nm at the limits of red. (A nano-metre is a thousanth of a millionth of a metre. (1/1000,000,000 or 10 to power –9)).

In the retina at the back of the eye there are two kinds of receptor cell which respond to the light which is focused on them by the lens. These are the "rods", (so named because of their shape), which are responsible for colourless vision in conditions of dim illumination, and the "cones" which operate at higher light levels and are responsible for colour perception.

At both ends of the visible band of wavelengths large energies of light are required to stimulate vision. However the eye is very sensitive to the wavelengths in the middle of the range, i.e. between 505nm, to which the rods are supremely sensitive, and 555nm, which is the area of peak sensitivity for the cones. These wavelengths are normally seen as green and yellowish green (lime).

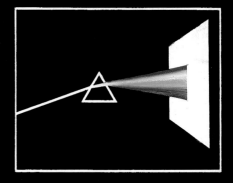

When a beam of white light is shone through a glass prism the various wavelenghts are bent (refracted) by differing amounts. They spread out and form a multicoloured spectrum which can be seen if a screen is placed in their path. The order of the colours is always the same: violet, blue, green, yellow, orange, red. No doubt you have noticed this order occurring naturally every time you have seen a rainbow.

Separating the colours of the visible spectrum.

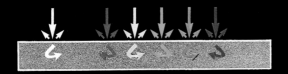

When light strikes a white surface most of it is reflected. (About 85% from a good white paper).

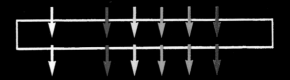

When light strikes a black surface most of it is absorbed. (About 4% is reflected from black ink).

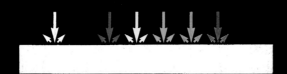

When light strikes a gray surface some is reflected and some is absorbed.

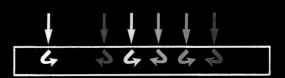

When light strikes a clear transparent surface it passes through.

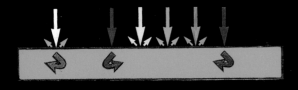

An opaque coloured surface selectively absorbs some frequencies of the spectrum and reflects others. In this example a green substance absorbs most light in the areas of red and violet but reflects more yellow, green and cyan.

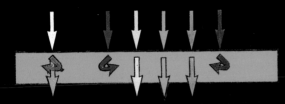

A transparent coloured material selectively absorbs some wavelengths and permits others to pass through.

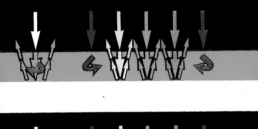

The coloured inks used in this book are transparent. Some light is absorbed (filtered); the remainder passes through and is reflected by the white paper. The light which is reflected to the eye has passed through the ink twice.

Red ink absorbs green, cyan and violet.

Cyan ink absorbs red and yellow.

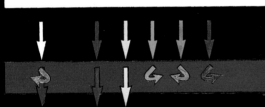

This diagram shows a red transparent ink printed over a cyan ink. * The wavelengths which pass through the red layer are absorbed by the cyan. Little light is reflected so the area of overprint looks black to the eye.

Fold the binary window (from page 3) in half and look through both filters. Once again the area of overlap is dark because most light is absorbed by one or other of the two coloured layers.

* In this book, as in most printing for coloured illustrations, red is not made by a single impression of ink. Rather it is made by overprinting yellow and magenta. (see page 8)

Colour Classification

Most methods of classifying colours use three principal variables.*

1. HUE: the difference between pure colours which is indicated by the names red, orange, green, blue, purple etc.; the principal difference caused by separating the component wavelengths of white light. The range from red to violet can be set out along a straight line. However, such a straight run does not accord with the obvious but curious fact that the red at the extreme end of the visible spectrum appears to have greater similarity to violet at the other end than to blue, green or cyan, all of which are closer to red in wavelength. It also leaves out hues such as magenta and purple. These do not appear with the other colours in the rainbow because they are mixtures of the two ends of the spectrum. However they are just as distinctive and vivid to the eye. The simplest way to resolve these difficulties is to curve the range of rainbow hues round the larger part of a circle. This puts red and violet closer to each other. The range of pure hues is then extended by inserting the non-spectrum hues between red and violet. This completes the circle.

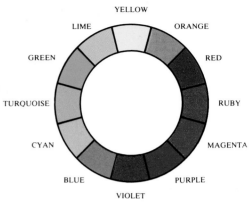

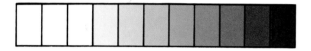

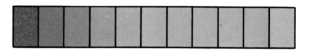

2. BRIGHTNESS: the range from light to dark.

This scale of grays is the simplest brightness sequence since hues are not present. However a range from any light colour to any dark colour is also a brightness scale

3. INTENSITY: the range from any pure hue to any point of the gray scale.

Intensity scales are of three principal kinds:

a) Tints: the range from a pure hue to white.
b) Shades: the range from a pure hue to black.
c) Tones: the range from a pure hue to any gray.

The diagram on the left shows the circle of pure hues with scales of tints and shades.

In order to include the larger number of tones a three-dimensional arrangement is used such as the one on the opposite page.

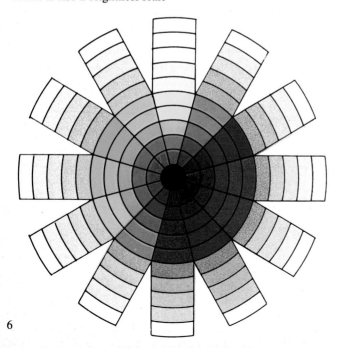

* Precise use of terms varies between authorities. Some seek to distinguish between light emissions and pigmentary reflections by using different sets of three terms. This is confusing in the view of the author, but you will encounter it in other books, so the most common variations are set out below.

		LUMINOSITY, BRILLIANCE or BRIGHTNESS	
LIGHT	– HUE		SATURATION
LIGHT or PIGMENT	– HUE	BRIGHTNESS	INTENSITY or SATURATION
PIGMENT	– HUE	VALUE	CHROMA

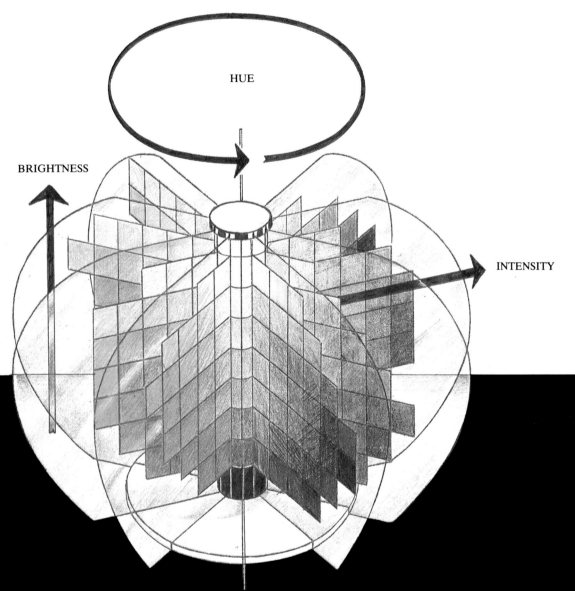

HUE

BRIGHTNESS

INTENSITY

This illustration shows a three-dimensional set of sample colours. The brightness scale runs vertically. The hue circle runs round the outside, and scales of intensity run horizontally. Many such "colour solids" exist but the basic three variable format is similar in most of them. They are used to specify colours exactly so they can be matched by designers, paint or dye manufacturers etc.

This one was designed by an artist, Albert H. Munsell, at the beginning of this century. It has been updated continually and is still in use as one of the best systems. The steps between neighbouring colour patches are visually equal and this means that the shape of the solid is not symmetrical. Yellow is the lightest pure hue, and is placed higher in relation to the brightness scale. Violet

Colour Mixing and Primary Colours

When mixing colours it is sometimes important to be able to employ a minimum number of basic hues to create a much larger range. In your art class at school, for example, you may have been told to use red, yellow and blue paints as primary colours. However only one of these primaries is correct for colour printing by modern methods.

The colours in this book have been printed using inks of magenta, yellow and cyan. On a circle of twelve hues these should be placed at equal distances from each other so as to form an equilateral triangle.

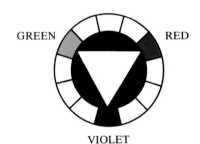

However the hues which are best for printing are not the same as the colours which are fundamental to human vision, or which are most effective for colour matching when projected beams of light are used. In this connection there is no simple answer to the question: "What are the primary colours?"

In the pioneering light mixing experiments of Thomas Young, published in 1802, and those of Helmholtz later in the 19th century, beams of red, green, and violet light were used. In this book these hues are still named as the "additive primaries" because they provide the best symmetry with the other three primaries which must be used for printing. For light mixing the most used alternative set which is employed extensively for scientific classification is red (or orange red), green, and blue (or bluish violet). You will find a note about the science of primaries on page 12.

On the colour circle the additive primaries also form a triangle.

When coloured light beams are projected onto a screen the areas of overlap are called additive mixtures. The results of overprinting transparent coloured inks are called subtractive mixtures.

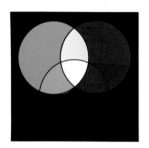

GREEN   yellow   RED
cyan   white   magenta
VIOLET

Additive mixing.
Three primaries
overlap to make white.

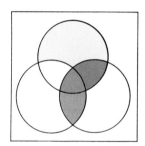

HUE
tint   tone   shade
WHITE   grey   BLACK

The relationship
between tints,
tones and shades.

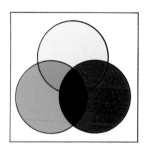

YELLOW
green   black   red
CYAN   violet   MAGENTA

Subtractive mixing.
Three primaries
overlap to make black.

Additive mixing is so called because each new superimposed colour adds to the brightness of the mixture. In subtractive mixing each new superimposed colour reduces the brightness of the mixture.

In additive colour mixing many combinations of three hues can be overlapped to make white and can be combined in different proportions to match all the remaining hues of the colour circle. The rule is that no combination of any two should match the third. However, in order to ensure that the mixed hues are vivid, intense colours, it is necessary to select primaries which are widely separated on the colour circle. As shown on the previous page this rule is satisfied by the choice of red, green and violet.

Partitive Mixture

There are other methods of mixing colours but most produce results which fall somewhere between additive and subtractive mixtures, or are combinations of the two.

For example pointillist mixtures are made when small dots of colour are placed together so that they seem to merge when viewed from a distance. In such dot mixtures the merged colours are neither darker nor lighter but appear as visual averages of the constituents.*

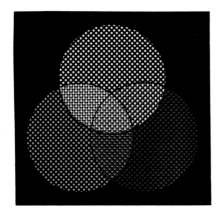

A pointillist mixture using the subtractive primaries. Stand the book vertically and view from a distance.

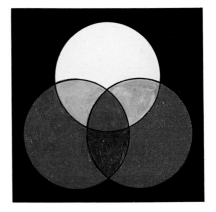

If you mix opaque pigments such as gouache or oil paint the results may be similar to the overlapped areas in this diagram. This is because some of the colouring agents are ground powders. The grains are too small to be seen by the naked eye but they act in a way which is similar to dots in determining the appearance of mixtures. Transparent dyes are also used in some paints and in most drawing inks. With these you should be able to mix primaries to make a good black, but you will have to work by trial and error to get the proportions exactly right.

* Similar effects can be produced with narrow stripes or other small shapes. The term "partitive mixture" is correct for such fusions because they involve tiny separations between the coloured areas.

Subtractive Mixing

Primaries:	Magenta	Yellow	Cyan			
Secondaries:	Red	Green	Violet			
*Tertiaries:	Orange	Ruby	Purple	Blue	Turquoise	Lime

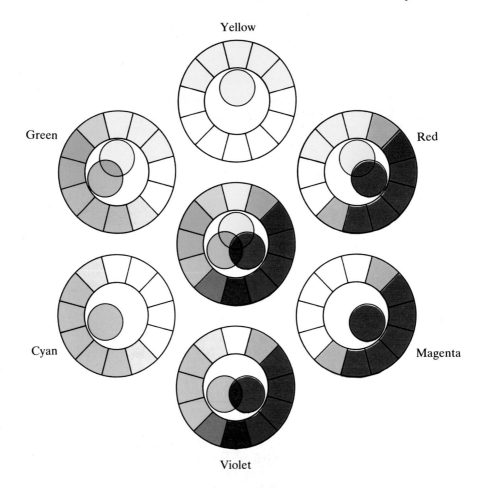

This set of circles shows how colour printing uses inks of three pure hues in various combinations to make the other colours by overprinting. You can see that the additive primaries red, green and violet can be made by overlapping different pairs of subtractive primaries. Most light is absorbed where all three overlap as in the central region of the middle circle which appears black although no black ink has been used, except for the lines.

  * A tertiary colour is a hue between a primary and a secondary. Another meaning, not used here, describes the colours made in pigments such as oil paint or watercolour when two secondaries are mixed. Such colours return to the primary hue but lose intensity and may be unpredictable in comparison with light mixtures or printing.

Additive Mixing

Primaries:	Red	Violet	Green			
Secondaries:	Yellow	Magenta	Cyan			
Tertiaries:	Orange	Ruby	Purple	Blue	Turquoise	Lime

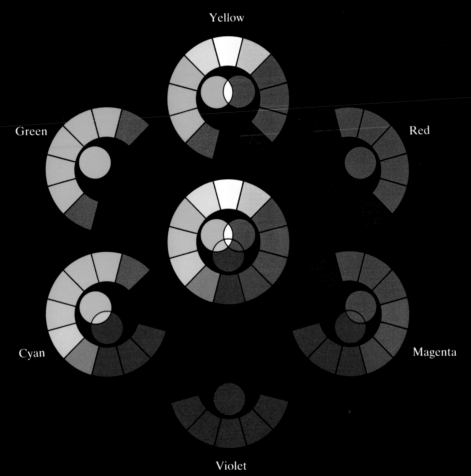

Yellow

Green

Red

Cyan

Magenta

Violet

For true additive mixing it is necessary to use lights, but these circles indicate how the three primaries can be combined in various proportions to make the other colours. In correct proportions pairs of additive primaries overlap to make the subtractive primaries. All three can be combined to make white.

Halftone Colour Printing

Printing which uses magenta, yellow and cyan inks is termed "trichromatic", or, when a plain black ink is added, it is called "four colour printing". If you use a magnifying glass to examine coloured pictures in most books and magazines you will see that they are made up of tiny dots printed in these three hues plus black.

To produce the twelve hues of most of the colour circles in this book, the trichromatic inks were used as follows:

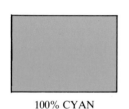

100% CYAN

	YELLOW	MAGENTA	CYAN
Yellow	100	0	0
Orange	100	40	0
Red	100	100	0
Ruby	40	100	0
Magenta	0	100	0
Purple	0	100	40
Violet	0	100	100
Blue	0	40	100
Cyan	0	0	100
Turquoise	40	0	100
Green	100	0	100
Lime	100	0	40

40% CYAN

The figures indicate the percentage of the coloured area which is covered by the ink of the dot matrix. Under a magnifier you will see dots on the colours with a 40 in one of the columns. 100% indicates a flat colour with no dots. The matrix is called "halftone" to distinguish it from graded or "continuous" changes in colour where no dots are used and many colours of paint or ink are required.

The Science of Vision and Primary Colours

The eye has three kinds of cone receptor which react selectively to different regions of the visible spectrum. These may be referred to by name as blue, green and red cones, but their regions of sensitivity are quite wide, overlap considerably, and the outer segments of the cells which react to light appear to have peak absorption at wavelengths of about 420 nm violet, 534 nm green and 564 nm yellow.* One way to calculate the degree to which each kind of cone contributes to the perception of any particular colour is to match the colour experimentally by stimulating the three types with three corresponding light beams mixed additively. For this purpose single wavelengths or narrow wavebands are employed but, for various reasons, the best wavelengths are not those to which the individual cones are most sensitive.

In the last few decades research has indicated that the nerve impulses from the three types of cone are not sent directly to the brain as signals indicating proportions of three primaries. Rather they are recombined by other cells in the retina and relayed to the brain as a brightness signal and two hue signals. One hue signal describes the amounts of red or green. The other describes the amounts of blue or yellow.

At the point where the nerve from the eye enters the brain is a small region called the lateral geniculate nucleus. It appears that here also are cells which react to opposite colour pairs rather than to one of three primaries. **

The cells are described by their reaction as:

a) Red Plus / Green Minus
b) Red Minus / Green Plus
c) Blue Plus / Yellow Minus
d) Blue Minus / Yellow Plus

The "Blue / Yellow" cells may actually have peak and minimum reactions in regions of the spectrum including bluish violet and orange but, like the "red" cones their names are now accepted. Whatever the exact wavebands involved it is established that they are roughly complementary, and this goes some way towards explaining the frequent occurance of complementary reactions in illusions and after effects.

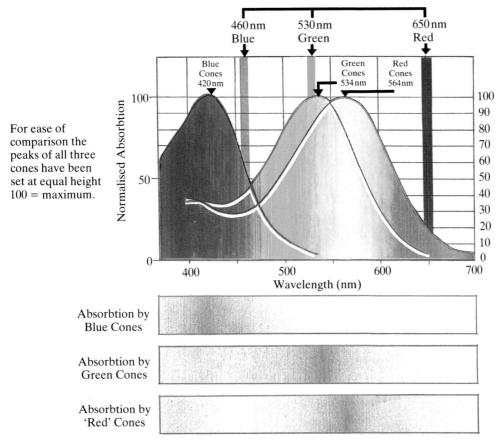

Typical wavelengths used in Additive Mixing experiments

* Research by Bowmaker and Dartnall, 1980. Other scientists report peak absorption at wavelengths which are slightly different.

** 1958 and 1966 R. L. De Valois and colleagues, work on macaque monkeys which have similar vision to humans.

Mixing by Spinning

When colours affect a region of the eye in rapid succession they appear to merge. This happens when you spin the discs on the opposite page and look steadily at the effect they produce. Your eyes cannot follow rotation so you see a mixture which is a visual average of the constituent colours. Unlike what occurs with additive or subtractive mixtures there is no general lightening or darkening of an area of overlap. Thus mixing by spinning is similar to pointillist mixing and is another form of partitive mixture. Whereas dot mixtures are partitive in space, spun colour mixtures are partitive in time.* All these discs are for rapid rotation using the spinners (from page 41).

1A   Although this wheel is exactly half black and half white it does not produce a mid gray when spinning. Compare the result with the gray scale on page 6 and you will see that it is much lighter than the point which is half way between black and white.

1B   Each concentric circle contains half the percentage area of the circular band inside it, yet the gray steps produced appear roughly even to the eye. Which band has the right proportion of black and white to mix to mid gray?

2A   Equal areas of three printed primaries do not mix by spinning to give a neutral gray. The brighter hues dominate. Thus the rotated mix of yellow, magenta and cyan looks yellowish. Red and green are lighter than violet in the additive set so they also mix to a tone which is slightly yellow. It is darker than the tone made by spinning the other three primaries because the constituents are darker.

2B   This wheel shows that it is possible to get closer to a neutral gray by altering the proportions of the colours in the mixture.

3A   Yellow and violet are complementary, i.e. colours which are opposite to each other (See page 17). Mixed in equal areas yellow predominates.

3B   Red and cyan are also complementary. On this disc they mix in all possible ratios. There is a region where they produce gray.

4A   Since red and cyan are closer to each other in brightness than the yellow / violet pair the colour produced by spinning equal areas is closer to gray.

4B   Lime is complementary to purple. On this wheel the gray areas reduce the dominance of the lighter colour.

* Early experiments in colour mixing and matching by means of rotating discs were made by James Clerk Maxwell in the 19th century.

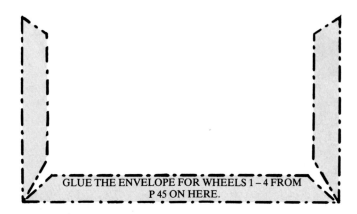

GLUE THE ENVELOPE FOR WHEELS 1 – 4 FROM P 45 ON HERE.

Wheels to illustrate mixing by spinning

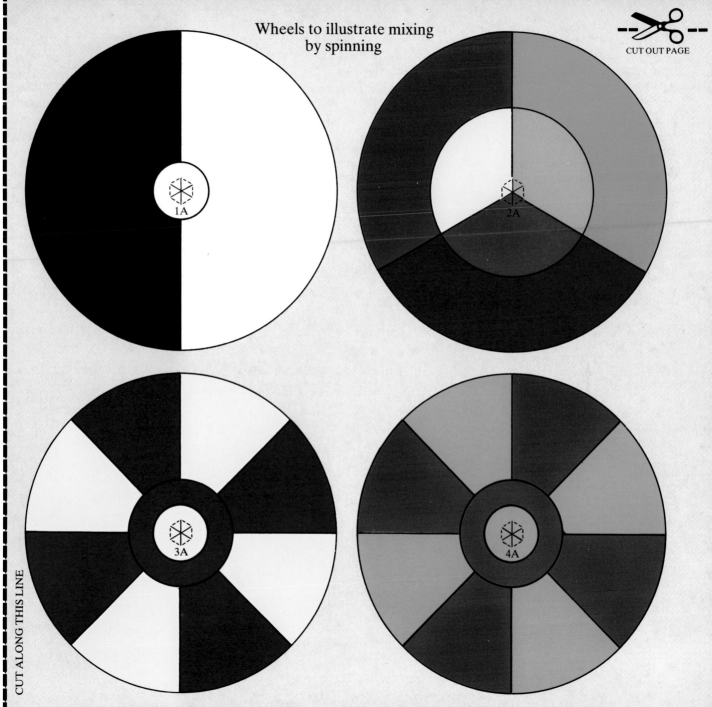

1A

2A

3A

4A

Cut out these mixing by spinning wheels while facing this page and store them in the envelope on page 14.

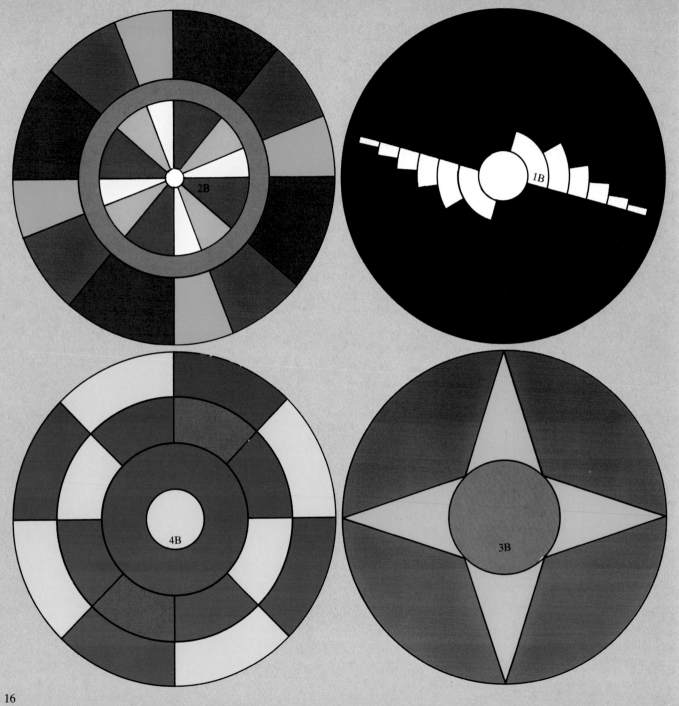

Complementary Colours and After Effects

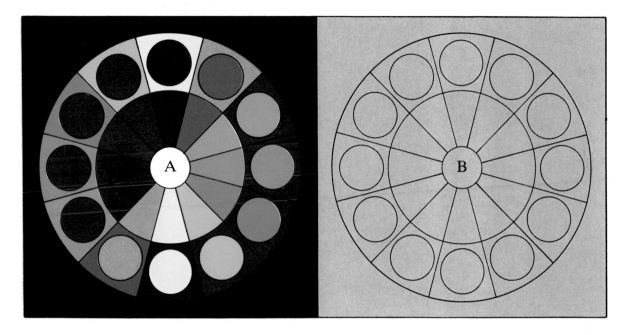

Complementary hues can be mixed to white by addition, black by subtraction and to gray or white by partition.* They are pairs of colours which are as different from each other as possible. On most colour circles they are placed opposite to each other. They produce each other as after effects.

Stare fixedly at centre A in the diagram above. Try to keep your eyes stationary for about 30 seconds then transfer your gaze to centre B in the blank circle. You will see an after image in which all the complementary colours exchange places. Another name for this phenomenon is successive contrast.

The choice of complimentaries on this page is based on subtractive printing as explained on pages 8 and 10. For additive mixing, colour diagrams place yellow opposite to blue or bluish violet. If you pay particular attention to the after effects of blue, violet and yellow in these diagrams you can see for yourself which colours are opposite to each other in perception.

The complementary hues are:

Yellow	Orange	Red	Ruby	Magenta	Purple
Violet	Blue	Cyan	Turquoise	Green	Lime

* Usually white can only be mixed partitively when the ingredients are luminous as they are, for example, in the screen of a television. In TV pictures dots of red, blue and green are mixed partitively to make all the other colours.

The Wheel of Harmony

Harmonious colours are those which look agreeable together. Theories of colour harmony seek to define general rules by which beautiful or effective colour combinations can be selected. Some artists and designers find such theories useful, others invent their own rules.

The principles of musical harmony largely depend on the mathematical relationships between sound wavelengths from different octaves. An octave is the span between one sound and another which is double or half the wavelength. The human ear can hear about 10 octaves. As stated on page 4 the visible spectrum extends between wavelengths of about 380 nm at the limits of violet light and 760 nm at the limits of red, scarcely a single octave. Therefore theories of harmony in colour are inevitably limited in comparison with ideas based on harmony in sound. In spite of this, Hermon van Helmholz tried to link sound and colour vibrations and many composers and artists have experimented with the ideas.

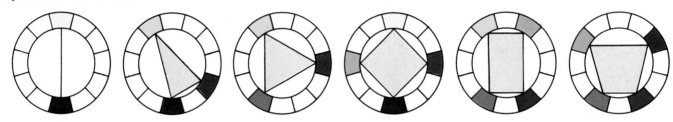

Many authorities have looked at the placement of colours on the colour circle and have drawn geometric figures between positions to indicate the symmetry of such relationships. Complementary pairs are placed opposite each other so their relationship is symmetrical. Groups of three primaries are symmetrical, as are all the groupings shown on these circles. According to such theories all these sets are harmonious.

SIDE A of the harmony wheel consists of a colour circle and a fan which has the same scheme. By turning the fan you can put any two pure colours together. At all times the twelve pairs produced will show the same relationship. The degree of displacement is indicated by the clock dial which appears through the window in the fan.

The following relationships are useful for creating harmonious colour schemes:*

| Same colour | Adjacent colours | Complementaries | Displaced Complementaries | Primaries and colours with similar degrees of displacement | Secondary to primary relationships and colours with similar degrees of displacement |

* The most influential works on simultaneous contrast, and effects of harmony include the writing and diagrams of Eugène Chevreul in the last century, Johannes Itten 1961 and Josef Albers 1963.

CUT OUT PAGE

The Wheel of Harmony

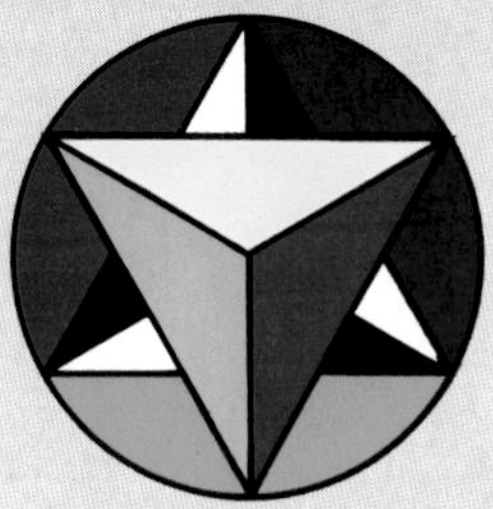

Hub cap to be glued over the centre of the fan on this page.

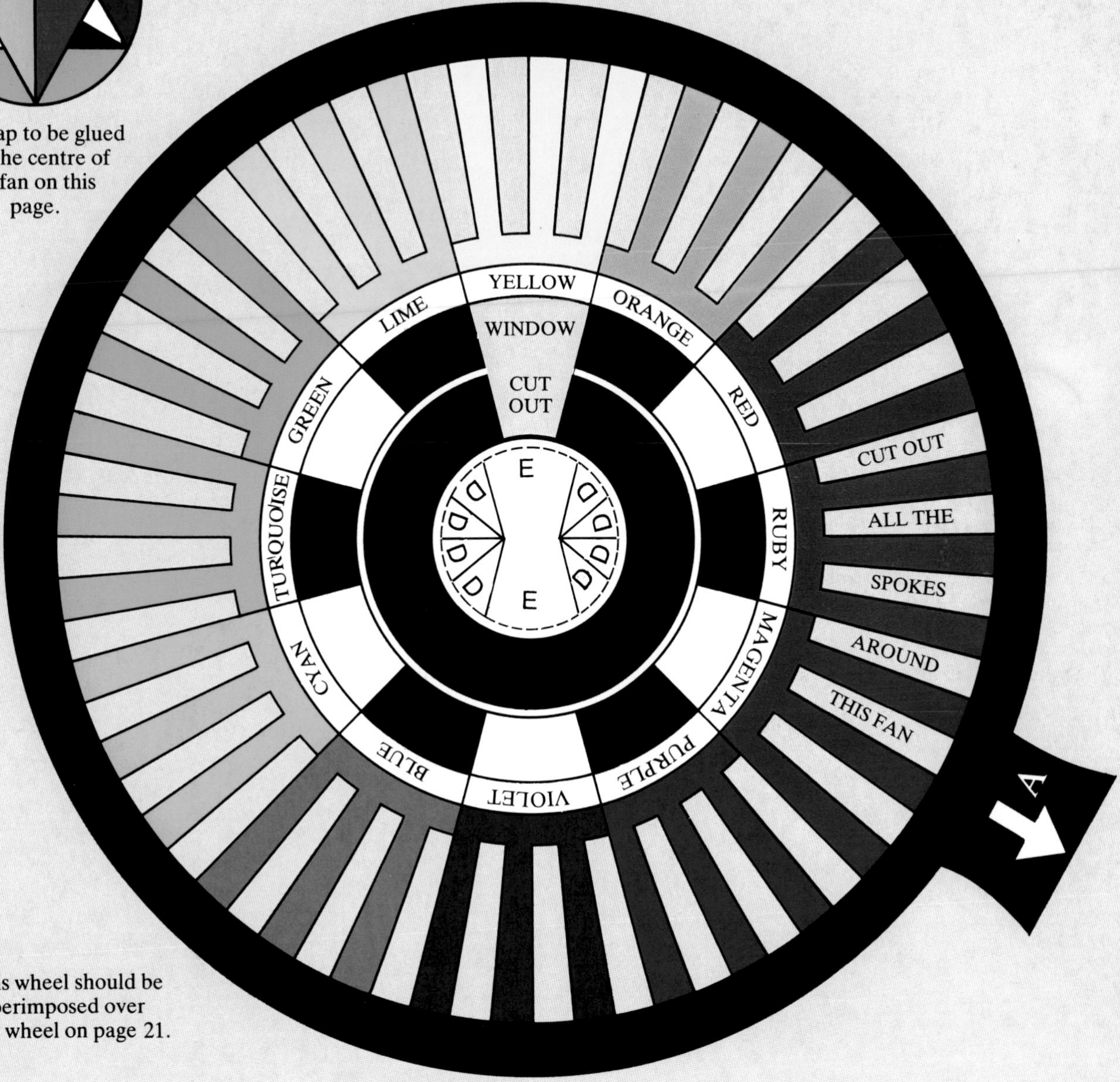

YELLOW
ORANGE
RED
RUBY
MAGENTA
PURPLE
VIOLET
BLUE
CYAN
TURQUOISE
GREEN
LIME
WINDOW
CUT OUT
CUT OUT
ALL THE
SPOKES
AROUND
THIS FAN
E
D
A

This wheel should be superimposed over the wheel on page 21.

CUT ALONG THIS LINE

The instructions for making the wheel of harmony are on page 40.

The Wheel of Harmony

This wheel should be
superimposed over
the wheel on page 21.

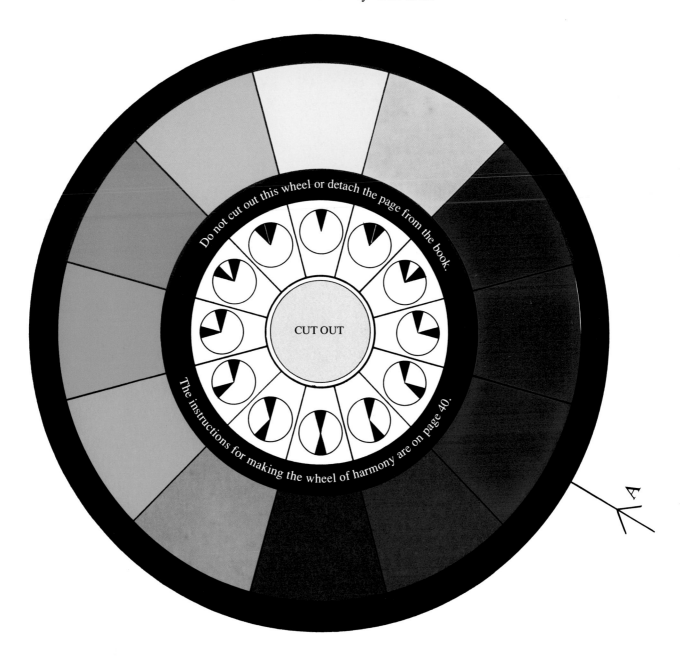

Do not cut out this wheel or detach the page from the book.

CUT OUT

The instructions for making the wheel of harmony are on page 40.

A

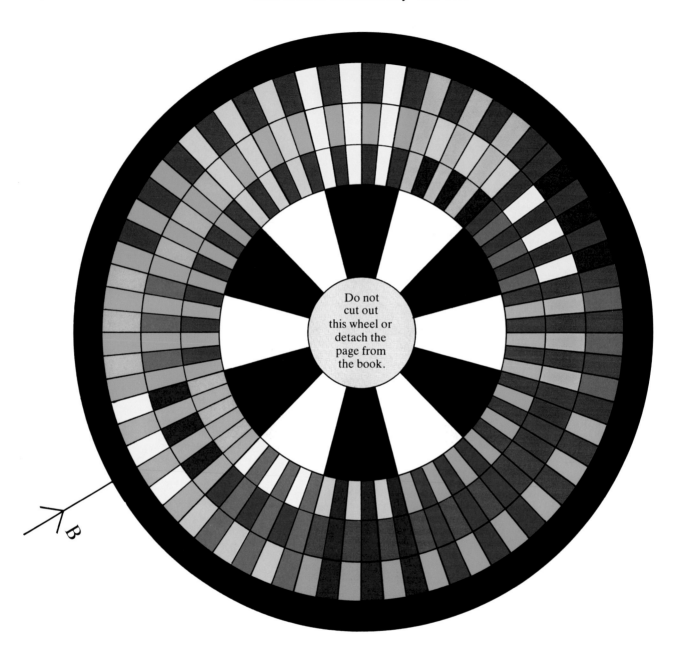

Do not
cut out
this wheel or
detach the
page from
the book.

B

The Wheel of Harmony

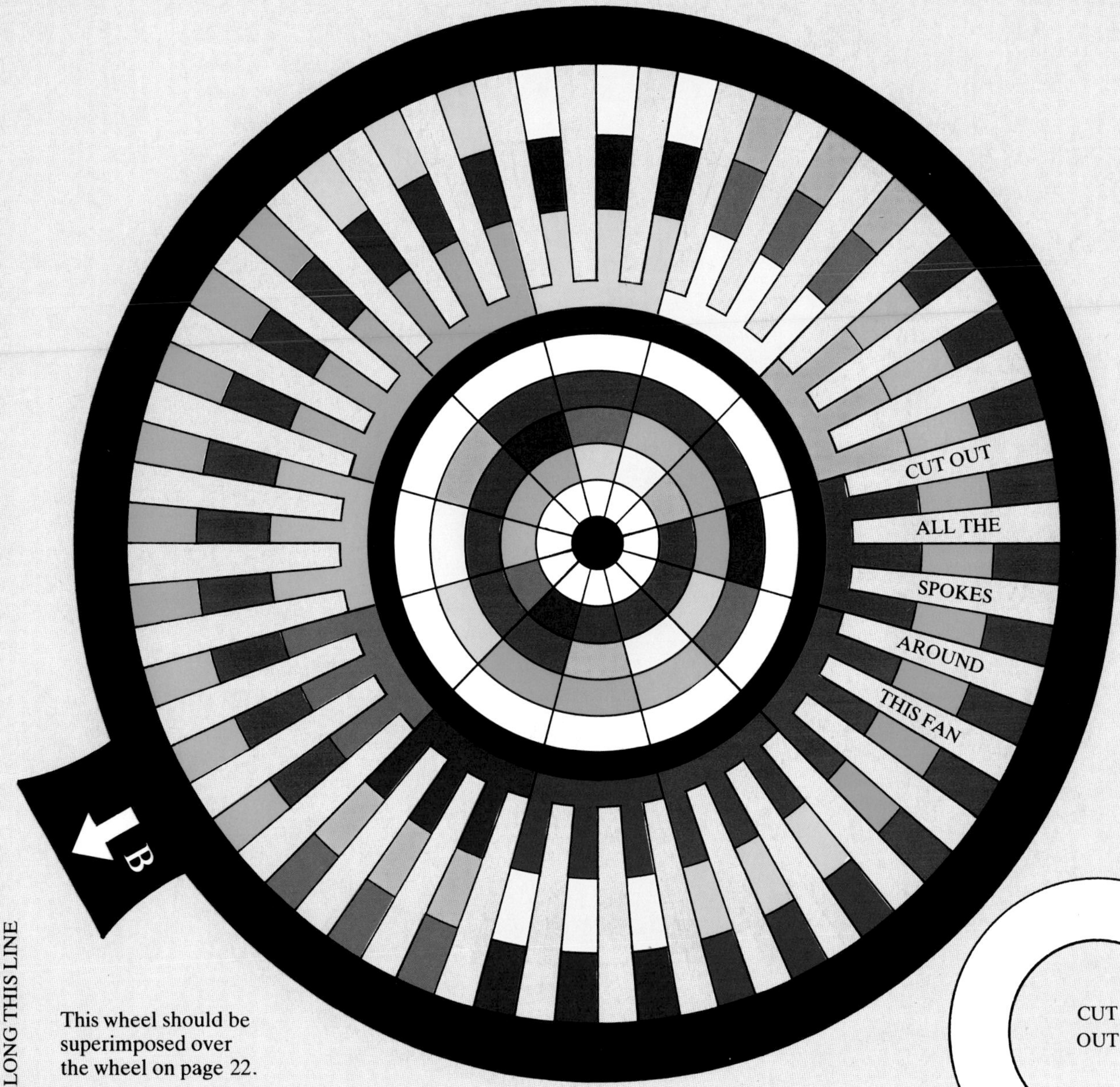

CUT OUT

ALL THE

SPOKES

AROUND

THIS FAN

B

CUT ALONG THIS LINE

This wheel should be
superimposed over
the wheel on page 22.

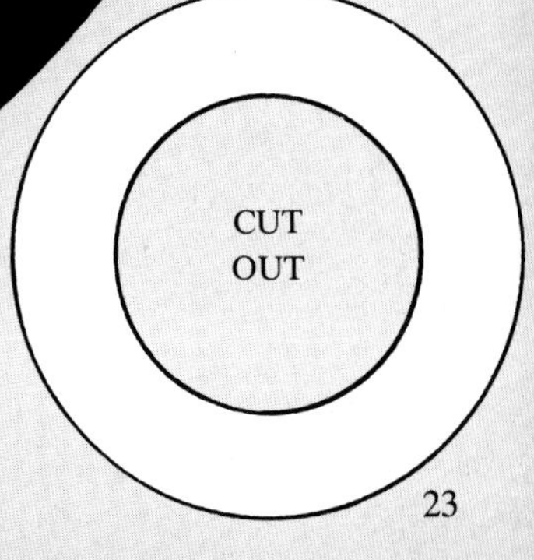

CUT
OUT

The instructions for making the wheel of harmony are on page 40.

23

The Wheel of Harmony

This wheel should be
superimposed over
the wheel on page 22.

The Wheel of Harmony

Other ideas about colour rely on the fact that similar colours go well together.

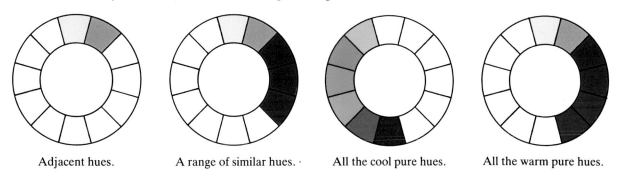

Adjacent hues.   A range of similar hues. ·   All the cool pure hues.   All the warm pure hues.

The four schemes below combine aspects of similarity (shown in the stepped or graduated sequences of the horizontal relationships), and strong contrast (shown in the large differences of the vertical relationships).

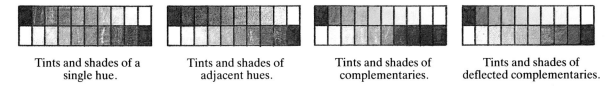

Tints and shades of a single hue.   Tints and shades of adjacent hues.   Tints and shades of complementaries.   Tints and shades of deflected complementaries.

These types of scheme were used by Post-Impressionist painters such as Van Gogh and Seurat; and by "Op" artists such as Vasarely and Bridget Riley.

SIDE B of the harmony wheel shows a more complex scheme as described in this diagram. Here one of the twelve segments of the wheel is shown. The colours of the other eleven segments maintain the same relationships round the complete colour circle. The fan has the same scheme as the wheel except that the wheel has an additional colour between the spokes, and the deflected complementaries are different. Within the limitations of trichromatic printing all the hues are shown at full intensity.

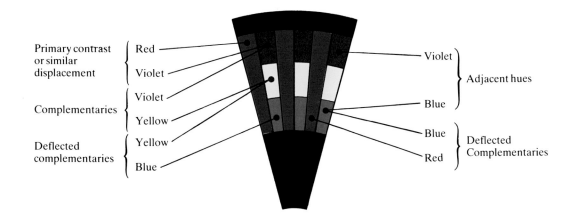

Primary contrast or similar displacement { Red — Violet —
Complementaries { Violet — Yellow —
Deflected complementaries { Yellow — Blue —

Violet — } Adjacent hues
Blue —
Blue — } Deflected Complementaries
Red —

Contrast and Assimilation

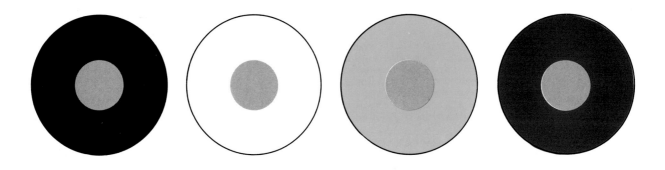

The gray patches in the centre of these circles are identical. However an illusion occurs which makes them appear to be different. When surrounded by black gray looks lighter than it does on a white background. Against red gray looks slightly cyan, while it looks slightly reddish when the background is cyan. This effect is called simultaneous contrast. It is similar to the effect of after image which we saw on page 17 in that the complementary rule always applies. In successive contrast we see the complementary after gazing at a patch of colour. In simultaneous contrast the opposite colour is seen while we are looking at the colour patches.

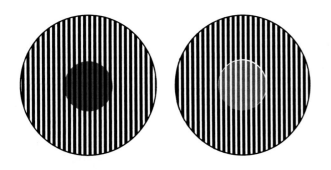

The red stripes in the centres of these two circles are printed in identical coloured inks. On the right the red alternates with white and looks lighter than it does on the left where it is spaced between black. This effect is called colour assimilation.

Note that the colours of the alternate stripes seem to bleed into each other despite the fact that we can still see the stripes distinctly. In the pointillist mixture on page 9 the colours blend totally when viewed from such a distance that the dots are too small to see. Despite this difference of scale, assimilation is a similar effect to optical mixture. It is precisely the reverse of the contrast illusions above.

In the illustration on the opposite page only four colours are used; black, white, red and cyan. If you view the colours from a distance, it becomes hard to believe that only one shade of red is used and only one shade of cyan. Assimilation is one of the strongest of all colour illusions.

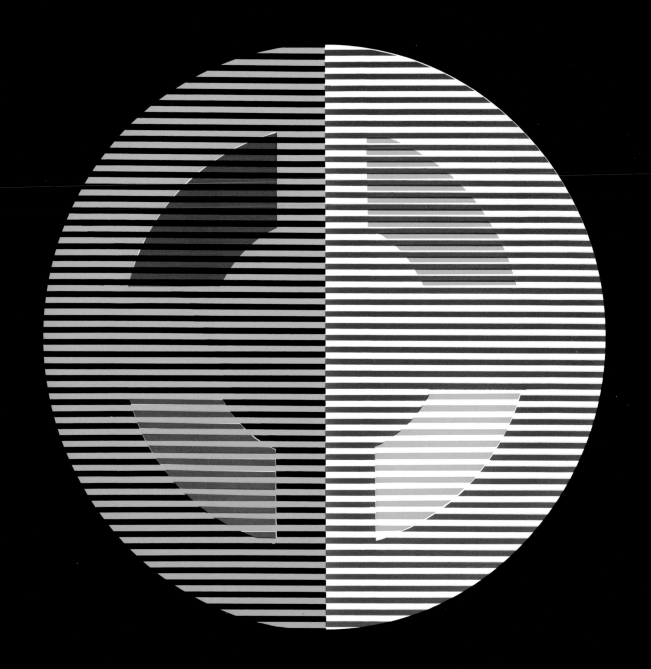

Kinetic Effects

Turn wheels 5 and 6 on the end of a pin or compass point.

5A On page 11 it was mentioned that pairs of additive primaries can be mixed additively to make subtractive primaries. For example yellow can be mixed by superimposing beams of green and red light. In a book it is impossible to demonstrate light effects but this disc shows something similar. When rotated slowly the blending effect of colour assimilation is enhanced by motion and the wheel appears as a complete colour circle which includes magenta, cyan and yellow.

5B Rotate slowly clockwise and notice that the wedges on the outer part of the disc appear flecked with yellow. At the same time the wedge shapes on the inner part of the disc seem to be edged with blue. When rotated anticlockwise the colours reverse. This illusion occurs because the motion reveals an effect which our eyes ignore in normal circumstances.

The lenses in our eyes act as prisms which focus the red and violet ends of the spectrum at slightly different distances from the retina. When we are looking at black and white designs this causes small rainbows to appear at the edges. If you look through a prism you will see the effect clearly because of the exaggerated refraction of the glass. In normal circumstances our eyes are able to ignore the lesser effect caused by the lens alone. However the motion confuses the way the edge contrasts are processed by the retina, so the rainbow effects become visible. Various after effects are also involved which do not involve refraction spectra. This was proved in 1948 by E. Gehrcke who demonstrated that colours are still seen even under illumination of a single wavelength. You can test this for yourself if you view the rotating disc under sodium street lighting.

Comparable designs are known as Benham's tops, and illusory colours from this type of black and white design are called Fechner Subjective Colours after Gustav Fechner, a scientist who researched into their cause.

6A Rotate slowly and view alternately through the red and cyan sides of the binary window. You will see the spirals expand and contract in turn, after prolonged viewing of a contracting spiral an expanding after effect is seen. This is known as a waterfall effect. Motion after illusions such as this were known to the Greek philosopher Aristotle (384 – 322 B.C.).

6B Rotate slowly and view through the binary window. When seen alternately through red and cyan filters two separate patterns appear which seem to behave differently. Straight lines seem to curve and different parts of the patterns are seen to blur and then become clear.

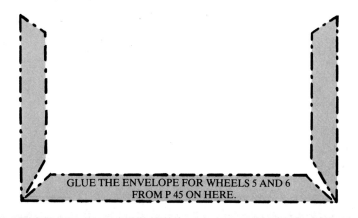

GLUE THE ENVELOPE FOR WHEELS 5 AND 6
FROM P 45 ON HERE.

Wheels to illustrate kinetic effects

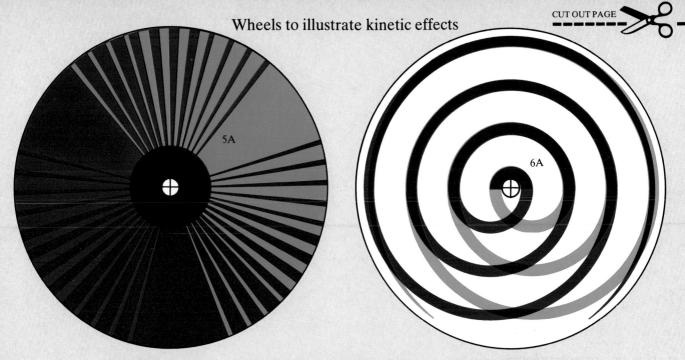

Cut out these kinetic effect wheels while facing this page and store them in the envelope on page 28.

Wheels to illustrate Cornsweet illusions

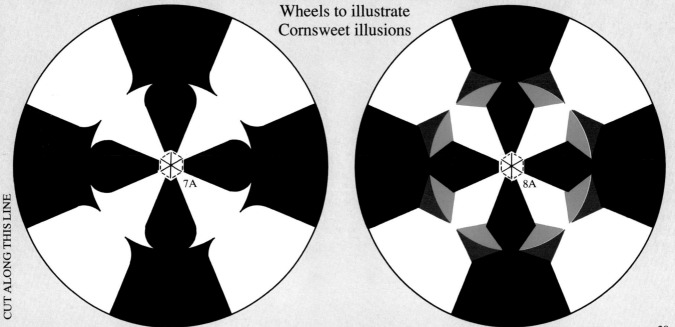

Cut out these Cornsweet illusion wheels while facing this page and store them in the envelope on page 31.

CUT ALONG THIS LINE

The Cornsweet Illusion *

Wheels 7 and 8 should be spun by using one of the spinners on page 41.

7A and 7B   On both sides of this wheel most of the area is sectioned with 50% black and 50% white. This produces a light gray when spinning. However the spurs create regions of contour contrast like this:

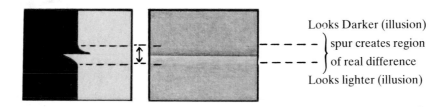

Looks Darker (illusion)
} spur creates region
} of real difference
Looks lighter (illusion)

On either side of the spur the gray looks different.

8A and 8B   In these variations of the Cornsweet illusion the effects are changed by viewing alternately through the red and cyan sides of the binary window.

* Named after T.N. Cornsweet as a particular example of this type of contrast illusion which was investigated in 1940 by Kenneth Craik and in 1958 by Vivian O'Brien.

GLUE THE ENVELOPES FOR WHEELS 7 and 8
FROM P 45 ON HERE.

The Transforming Iris

This device is based on a Victorian idea for creating transforming scenes in "pop-up" books. On both sides it creates dramatic effects of alternation in colour. Like the other illusions in this book where rotation is involved the Transforming Iris makes its impact through the interaction of motion and pattern. It exploits the fact that the perception can be confused by complicated patterns similar to those used in mazes, "Op Art" and some types of visual puzzle.

In nature similar designs have evolved for different purposes including display, warning, camouflage and species identification. The stripes of the zebra, the patterns on butterfly wings and the markings on insect attracting flowers are all examples of this kind of confusing or startling design.

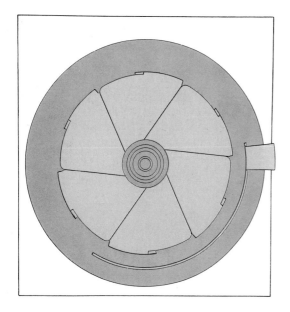 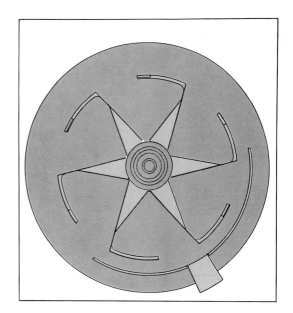

As you can see from these outline diagrams the cut shape of the Iris is quite simple. However the printed design contradicts or disguises the actual edges so that the changing phases are as difficult to follow as a conjuring trick. To produce the changes just move the handle to and fro along the curved slit.

If you look at the colour schemes of the circles and wheels explained on pages 14 to 25 you may be able to work out how the principles of colour similarity and contrast have been used to enhance the optical changes which are produced by the Iris. The design also incorporates the broken spiral effect of the spinning tops, and has opposing angles which have some similarity to the angular contrasts exploited on Wheel 6B.

Do not cut out this disc or detach the page from the book.

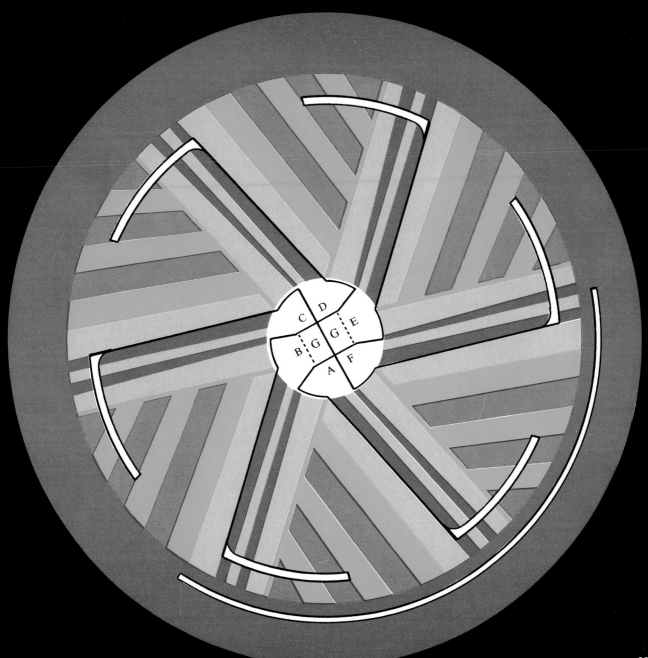

The Transforming Iris

The Transforming Iris

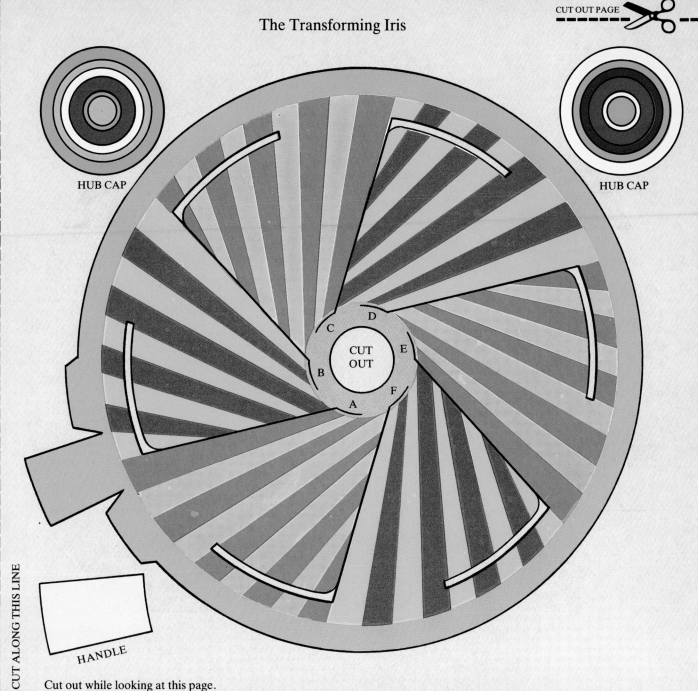

HUB CAP

HUB CAP

HANDLE

Instructions for assembly are on page 47.

Cut out while looking at this page.

CUT ALONG THIS LINE

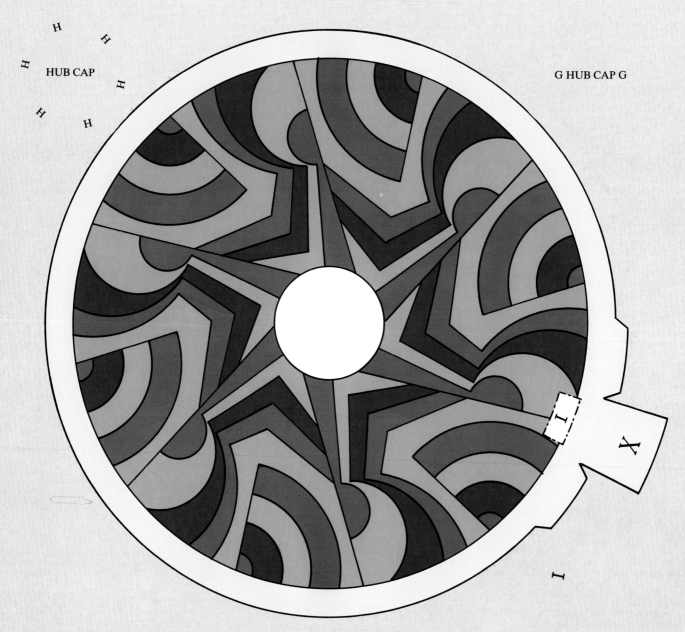

The Transforming Iris

Cut out while looking at page 35.

The Stroboscopic Disc

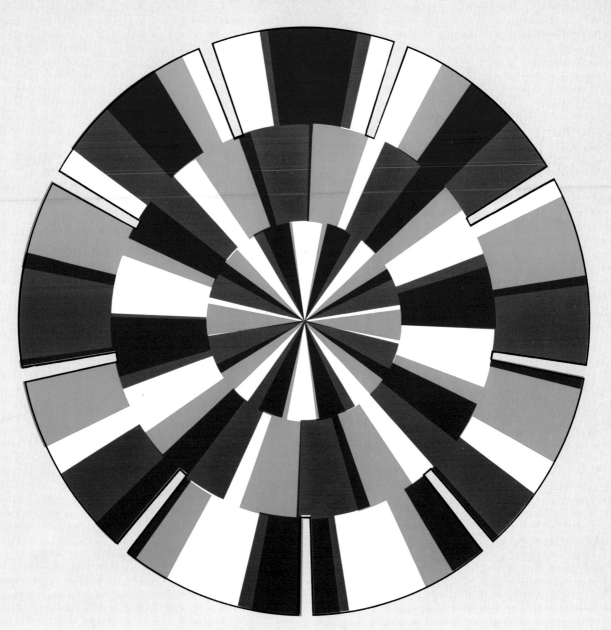

Cut out while looking at this page.

Cut out while looking at page 37.

KEEP YOUR STROBOSCOPIC DISC IN HERE

The stroboscopic disc is also an adaptation of a Victorian device which was used both scientifically and as an intriguing toy. Mount the disc on the end of a pin or compass point so that it will turn freely. Hold it up in front of a mirror in such a position that you can look at the reflection through the cut slits at the edge. Spin the disc rapidly and you will see an effect of apparent rotation which is different in speed or direction from the actual movement. Both sides of the disc will produce this stroboscopic effect.

If you view the spinning reflection alternately through the red and cyan filters of the binary window you will see the illusion separate into clockwise and anticlockwise directions. This will happen whichever way you turn the wheel.

Stroboscopic devices work by presenting a series of images to the eye in rapid succession. Each picture or design is viewed momentarily as part of a sequence. If the series is suitable it is perceived as a continuous moving picture because our brains fill in the gaps. This fused motion is similar to the colour fusion by spinning described on page 14. In both cases a succession is perceived as a continuous event.

We can also think of the stroboscopic disc as a filter since the flanges block the view between the slits. The colour filters of the binary window act in a similar selective way by blocking and revealing different aspects of the whole picture. Such parallels or interactions between colour, shape and motion are of great interest to scientists who study visual perception.

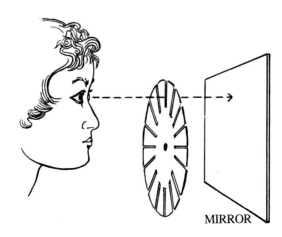

MIRROR

HOW TO MAKE THE WHEEL OF HARMONY

CUTTING OUT

1. Remove pages 19 and 23 from the book by cutting along the bold dotted lines.

Do not remove page 21

2. Looking at page 19, cut out all the spokes and the window.

3. Score and cut out the pivot teeth marked D at the centre of the wheel.

 —— CUT LINES
---- SCORE LINES

4. Cut out the wheel and the hub cap precisely.
5. Looking at page 23, cut out all the spokes around the wheel. Then cut out the wheel and the washer precisely.
6. Looking at page 21 and protecting the following pages of the book, cut out the centre of the wheel.

ASSEMBLY

1. Place the "A" wheel on page 21 and fold the pivot teeth down through the hole. Line up the A arrows.

2. On page 22 place the washer with its grey side uppermost so that the teeth come through the hole. Glue the teeth to the washer as indicated by the letters C.

3. Keeping the A arrows on page 21 lined up, glue the "B" wheel to the washer on page 22 so that the B arrows also line up.

4. As the glue dries, check that both the A and B arrows line up and that the wheels can turn freely.

5. Complete the wheel of harmony by glueing the hub cap into position on page 21.

HOW TO MAKE THE SPINNERS

1. Remove page 41 from the book by cutting along the bold dotted line.

2. Cut out both rectangles and score along the central dotted lines.

3. Fold each rectangle backwards in half and spread glue smoothly inside the fold. Press firmly and leave till dry.

4. Cut out each spinner precisely.

5. Select a piece of sharpened pencil 5cm. long for each spinner. A six-sided pencil is best.

6. Lightly score the small hexagons at the centre of each spinner and then cut the three slits.

7. Push the sharpened end of the short pencil through the centre of each spinner and then glue the six small triangles to the pencil.

8. Make sure that the pencils are at right angles to the faces of the spinner and then allow to dry.

Use the spinners with the colour wheels which are stored on pages 14, 28 and 31.

When you have finshed making up this book glue
the blue area on this page to the blue area on page 47.
This makes an envelope for the stroboscopic disc.

The spinners   The instructions for making the spinners are opposite.

**UNDER SIDE
OF SPINNER**

The design on the upper side of this spinner is based on broken
spirals. When spinning the degree to which the broken
spirals produce illusions of expansion or contraction
varies with speed.

**UPPER SIDE
OF SPINNER**

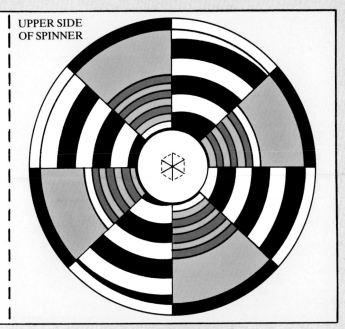

**UNDER SIDE
OF SPINNER**

The design on the upper side of this spinner is based on broken
spirals. When spinning the degree to which the broken
spirals produce illusions of expansion or contraction
varies with speed.

**UPPER SIDE
OF SPINNER**

CUT ALONG THIS LINE

Use these spinners with the wheels on pages 15, 16, 29 and 30.

A

A

B

B

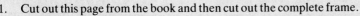

The Binary Window

A   B

CUT OUT   **CUT OUT**

CUT OUT   **CUT OUT**

GLUE RED FILTER HERE   GLUE CYAN FILTER HERE

A   B

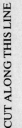

1. Cut out this page from the book and then cut out the complete frame.
2. Score along the lines marked – – – –
3. Cut out the four windows
4. Glue the red and cyan filters (from the title page) into position, taking care that the glue does not spread onto the window areas.
5. Fold towards you so that the letters A and B correspond.
6. Glue the frame together, taking care once again not to allow glue to stray onto the window areas.
7. Store the finished device in the pocket on page 3.

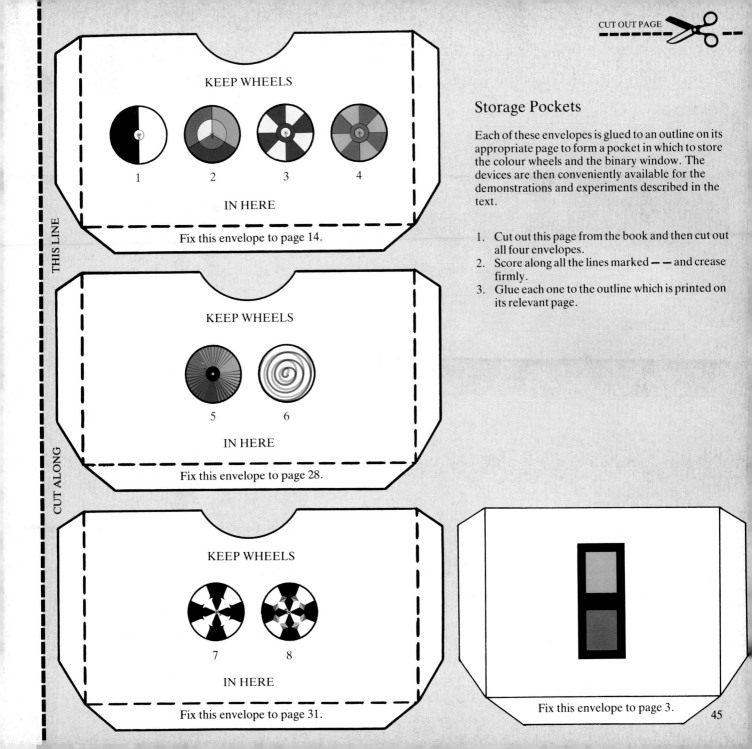

KEEP WHEELS

1   2   3   4

IN HERE

Fix this envelope to page 14.

THIS LINE

CUT ALONG

KEEP WHEELS

5   6

IN HERE

Fix this envelope to page 28.

KEEP WHEELS

7   8

IN HERE

Fix this envelope to page 31.

Storage Pockets

Each of these envelopes is glued to an outline on its appropriate page to form a pocket in which to store the colour wheels and the binary window. The devices are then conveniently available for the demonstrations and experiments described in the text.

1. Cut out this page from the book and then cut out all four envelopes.
2. Score along all the lines marked — — and crease firmly.
3. Glue each one to the outline which is printed on its relevant page.

Fix this envelope to page 3.

HOW TO MAKE THE TRANSFORMING IRIS

CUTTING OUT

1. Remove pages 35 from the book by cutting along the bold dotted line.

Do not remove page 33

2. Looking at page 33 and protecting the following pages of the book, cut along all lines and slots as shown in fig. 1. Score along the two short dotted lines.

3. Looking at page 35 cut along all lines and slots as before and cut out the central hole.

4. Cut out the wheel, handle and hub caps precisely.

ASSEMBLY

1. Place the cut-out wheel on to page 34, so that the "X" side is uppermost.

2. Slot the handle through as shown in fig. 2, which is the view from page 33.

3. Looking at page 33, place tab A through slit A as shown in fig. 3.

fig. 1

fig. 2

fig. 3

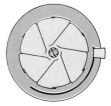

fig. 4

Wheel on page 33

Cut-out wheel

4. Place tab B through slit B and then continue clockwise with tabs C, D, E, F passing through slits C, D, E, F.

5. Carefully slide the handle to the other end of the handle slot as shown in fig. 4. Check that the wheels turn freely and smoothly when the handle is moved.

6. Fold the tabs G back over the grey circle and glue the tabs carefully to the appropriate hub cap. Be careful **not** to put any glue on to the grey circle. Turn to page 34 and glue the other hub cap into position using the six tabs H.

7. Glue the handle into position using the point I.

8. As the glue dries, check that the handle can move smoothly to either end of the handle slot.

When you have finished making up this book glue
the blue area on this page to the blue area on page 40.
This makes an envelope for the stroboscopic disc.